Made in United States
North Haven, CT
05 June 2025

69461550R10061